WHISPERS OF LIFE

CORNERS OF ROUND WORLD

NAVDEEP SOOD

Made with ♥ on the Notion Press Platform
www.notionpress.com

Dedication

To my mother, for your endless love.

To my father in heaven, for your guidance.

To my sister, for laughter and support.

To my wife, for teaching me love.
To my children, for joy and innocence.
To nature, for shaping my heart.

To my teachers, for your wisdom.

To the readers, with gratitude.
This book is for all of you.

Contents

Contents

Foreword

This book, *Whispers of Life*, is not just the work of one person, but a reflection of a family's love, encouragement and shared belief in the beauty of nature and above all *life's quiet lessons.* What began as Navdeep's personal reflections soon became a family mission, as those closest to him insisted it was time for his messages to be shared with the world.

Each family member played a part—Shally, with her unwavering enthusiasm, Usha's motherly pride, Nitika's boundless excitement, and the gentle reminders from Jigyasa and Shaurya of the power of listening to life's subtle messages. Across oceans, Yannik urging Deepu Mama to share the whispers that had inspired them all.

At the heart of this book lies the memory of Navdeep's father, his greatest mentor, who taught him to listen—to nature, to life, and to his heart. *Whispers of Life* is a tribute to these lessons and to the love that binds us, not just as family, but as caretakers of this beautiful world.

With love

The Sood Family

Preface

The whispers of life surround us, gentle yet persistent, like the soft rustling of leaves in a sunlit forest or the tranquil murmur of a stream. They communicate a timeless wisdom—one that reminds us how to love deeply, live fully, and grow with purpose. *Whispers of Life* is a collection inspired by these delicate yet powerful voices, guiding us toward the essential values that truly matter: love, connection, nature, and our role within the intricate web of existence.

In my professional life, I navigate the hum of technology, striving to bridge distances between people. Yet, my heart remains steadfastly connected to the wild, where I have dedicated over two decades to wildlife conservation. This journey is not merely a duty; it is a profound calling that has taught me to respect and nurture the natural world, reminding us that every creature plays a vital role in the circle of life.

Through my adventures in nature, I've encountered invaluable lessons about resilience, joy, and interconnectedness. The wild teaches us to appreciate the beauty of survival and the transformative power of love. It shows us that, much like an ecosystem, our lives flourish when we embrace compassion, understanding, and support for one another.

Whispers of Life is deeply rooted in the love of my family, who embody the essence of kindness and encouragement. They have illuminated the importance of standing together, celebrating small moments, and embracing life's challenges with grace. Their love inspires me to approach each day with an open heart, ready to discover beauty in both the ordinary and extraordinary.

This book serves as a tribute to those everyday lessons—most we already know, some we may have forgotten. It reminds us how to live life more fully, to embrace both selections and rejections, to take things in stride, and to understand the bigger picture. The most meaningful aspects of life often lie in the simplest moments: a parent's warm embrace, a child's laughter, the gentle call of a bird at dawn, and the wisdom found in the stillness of an ancient forest. These whispers guide us to appreciate what truly matters.

As you explore these pages, I invite you to listen closely to the whispers around you. Feel the heartbeat of the Earth beneath your feet, cherish the love that envelops you, and remember that we are all part of a greater story—one that calls us to respect, nurture, and protect the world we share.

May *Whispers of Life* inspire you to seek joy, embrace growth, and foster love in your life. Let it remind you that in every corner of this beautiful world, there are lessons to learn, connections to nurture, and love to share.

With deep gratitude and hope,

Navdeep Sood

29th November 2022

Tarn Taran

Acknowledgements

The creation of *Whispers of Life* has been a journey enriched by the support and inspiration of many loved ones. With heartfelt gratitude, I acknowledge those who have been integral to this work.

First and foremost, thank you to my family—who instilled in me the values of kindness and compassion, and whose unwavering love has been my guiding light. Thanking my caring sister, I especially honor my mother, whose lessons as a teacher have profoundly influenced me.

To my best friend and loving father, though you are no longer with me, your memory continues to inspire and guide me. I carry your dreams and wisdom in my heart.

To my wonderful wife, thank you for your endless patience and understanding as I spend time in the wild. Your support means the world to me.

To my children, your joy and enthusiasm are my greatest treasures. My daughter's pure love and my son's vibrant spirit uplift and ground me and their music rejunivates me. You are the heart of this book.

I extend a special thanks to the wildlife and natural world, especially the leopards and other creatures that have taught me invaluable lessons in resilience and beauty. The wild has been a profound source of inspiration for this endeavor.

To my friends, your encouragement and shared passion for making a difference have fueled my determination and creativity.

Thank you for believing in my work.

To the readers of this book, thank you for joining me on this journey. Your openness to exploring these whispers of life makes sharing these messages so rewarding.

Finally, my deepest appreciation goes to all who supported and believed in this project, including my teachers and the institutions where I studied. Your contributions have been crucial in bringing *Whispers of Life* to fruition.

With warmest regards,

Navdeep Sood

Prologue

To live life meaningfully is to embrace each moment, avoiding the blind rush that often pulls us away from what truly matters. *Whispers of Life* is a gentle reminder to slow down, breathe deeply, and immerse ourselves in the beauty of existence.

In these pages, you'll find inspiration to live fully and authentically. Embrace the calmness that surrounds us, respect one another, and cherish the natural world. Each lesson echoes the importance of connection—whether to loved ones or the earth itself.

Let this collection guide you toward a life filled with purpose, joy, and an appreciation for the whispers that call us to be present and alive.

With gratitude and hope,

Navdeep Sood

To Frost

In the realm of literature, few voices have resonated as deeply and enduringly as those of the great poets, among them Robert Frost. The poet, and many others whose works we encountered in our formative years, served as our guides through the rich landscapes of human experience and emotion. Their verses, akin to the films of today, unfurled before us like vivid scenes on a screen, creating images and impressions that have become timeless memories etched into our minds.

For our generation, these poems were not merely texts to be studied; they were a form of television, a medium through which we explored the world. The imagery and sentiments conveyed by these poets shaped our understanding of nature, life, and the human condition. Their words were as vivid and compelling as any visual media, providing us with a sense of connection and insight that was profound and lasting.

As the world around us evolves at a pace faster than ever, the challenges and circumstances we face are continually shifting. In light of this rapid change, we turn to the wisdom of these literary giants, like Robert Frost, whose work has guided and inspired countless readers. In the pages that follow, specifically in Chapters 29, 30, and 31, I pay tribute to Frost's original contributions and, with the deepest respect, present a request for his guidance as we navigate contemporary issues.

To honor the spirit of Frost's work, two new messages, crafted in response to the current state of our world have been included. These messages are presented with full acknowledgment of Frost's influence and originality. They are not intended to alter his legacy but to reflect the lessons we have learned from him and apply them to the new contexts we face today. The credit for the inspiration and foundation of these verses remains solely with Robert Frost, whose enduring words continue to light our path.

With heartfelt gratitude and reverence, I invite you to journey through these reflections in Chapters 29, 30, and 31 and witness how the timeless wisdom of Frost resonates with the modern era.

1. Corners of Round World

In our round world, corners everywhere,
Each one a space where love's light can flare.
If in any corner of this vast sphere,
A heart finds another to hold dear,
It's a blessing profound, a truth so clear,
A gift of love that draws us near.
The corners of round world defy all roles
The lines parallel at equator meet at poles.
For love is love, in every form it flows,
In corners near or far, where affection grows.
In its curves, paths interwine,
To find someone loving you is truly divine
So cherish the love, let it brightly gleam,
In every corner of this earthly dream.

2. Things Choose Us

I run after things my whole life,
Spending precious days in endless strife.
I work hard to gather what gleams and shines,
In hopes that joy will follow in its lines.
But every treasure, every fleeting gain,
Leaves me longing, still feeling the same.
Materials, mere tools for ease, we should see,
The door, the furniture, the window, the tree.
Once they lived, and maybe they still do,
A silent witness, a life passing through.
The life we shape that makes our way,
Was it aimed for us, or do we stray?
What if the land, the home, the key,
Were not things we chose, but chose to be?
What if each object, each path we take,
Was gently guiding the choices we make?
Do we mold life, or does life mold us?
In the end, who's really in control—
what if the things chose us?

3. I May Be Something

I may be something in this world, but...
My greatest joy is simple and clear,
Riding my bicycle each morning light,
Beside my son, whom I hold dear.
Love's journey matters, not what's seen.
In a world so tangled in wealth and pride,
I choose the road less paved with gold,
For bonds are built not in luxury's ride,
But in stories shared and hands to hold.
To teach my child of love's true worth,
Beyond the gleam of things and things,
I show him joy in every breath,
In laughter, wind, and simple springs.
I may have titles, status, and more,
But what good are they without the spark
Of mornings spent with those we adore,
Of hearts aglow that lights the dark.
So let us ride this humble path,
And plant the seeds of love so true,
For childhood's magic never lasts,
Unless it blooms with me and you.

4. Dance of Flow

Things may not unfold as we desire,
Life's dance is not a scripted choir.
Plans may falter, paths may bend,
But each twist holds a new transcend.
To force the flow is not the way,
Not every wave bends to our sway.
In rigid hands, we miss the grace,
Of nature's own, unfettered pace.
So let it be, let currents guide,
With open heart, embrace the tide.
Sometimes the best is to accept,
The universe's gift, precept.
Flow with the flow, let joy arise,
In what unfolds before your eyes.
Happily nudge, with gentle cheer,
For life's true dance is crystal clear.

5. Neon Symphony

Oh, how we dream of neon lights,
Perfumes rare, and skies so bright!
But in the gardens, wild and free,
A life unfolds more rich than we.
The humble fly, the busy bee,
Drenched in nature's symphony,
They dance through petals, soft and sweet,
In a world of color at their feet.
They taste the nectar, pure and true,
A feast of flavors, skies of blue.
Flashing lights from flowers bright,
More stunning than our neon night.
Their world hums with vibrant song,
They flit and flutter all day long.
In their buzzing, humming flight,
They work a magic out of sight.
For every sip of sweet delight,
They gift the world its fruits of life.
They pollinate, and with a wing,
Make fields bloom and harvest sing.
Imagine living for a day,
In this fragrant, dazzling play—

We'd see the gifts they truly bring,
And cherish every buzzing wing.
So next you see an insect small,
Remember, they are life for all.
Their party is our future bright,
Their world, a glowing, wondrous light.

6. Reverse

How we speak, for day and night align,
Male and female are one, in nature's design.
They are not opposites, though we claim it so—
Each needs the other; alone, they can't grow.
We say we'll save you, like we hold the key,
But you, with your mountains, your rivers, your sea,
Have weathered the ages, through storm and through flame—
It's we who are fragile, yet we speak your name.
You cradle us gently, yet we act so grand,
Forgetting our roots in your soil, your sand.
We beg now in earnest, no longer above—
"Dear Earth, please save us," with humility and love.
For you'll go on turning when we are no more,
With skies still as blue, and waves on your shore.
Let us be your children, respectful and wise,
And learn, before losing, to open our eyes.
And let us shift from "Let us save the Earth,"
To asking instead, "Dear Earth, Please Save Us."

7. Embrace the Wild

Step outside, feel the morning sun,
Let nature's wonders be your run.
Mountains high and rivers wide,
In nature's arms, find peace inside.
See the wild in the wild, untamed,
Where nature's raw and unframed.
Not caged, but roaming free,
In their freedom, find your glee.

8. Sit With The Self

Come, sit with the self beneath the noise,
Lay down the mask that hides your truth,
Feel the whisper the world destroys,
Reclaim the quiet of child in you.
In the hurried race, we often stray,
Burdened with roles that aren't our own,
Yet the soul calls softly, "Find your way,"
To the place where seeds of peace are sown.
We pass through Time, a river wide,
But pause and rest on its gentle shore,
Meet the true self you've kept inside,
And know yourself evermore.

9. Never Ever

The greatest sorrow in this world we find,
Is to cause pain to a heart so kind.
To wound the soul that gives with grace,
Is the deepest hurt we can ever face.
For love's pure light should never know,
The sting of hurt, the sharpest blow.
So cherish hearts that love so true,
And guard their peace, as they guard you.

10. Blank Pages

Precious are. God's blank pages bright,
Unwritten scrolls, pure and light.
Their hearts are canvases, wide and clear,
Awaiting gentle hands to steer.
Parents, view the roles you weave,
In every tale that they conceive.
If shadows fall on paths they tread,
Reflect on how you've gently led.
For if their stories wane or stray,
It's not their fault, but how you lay
The lines and hues upon their quest,
In every choice, in every test.
So write with love, with artful grace,
For you've begun their life's embrace.
With every stroke, with every start,
You shape their dreams and guide their heart.

11. Legacy

Teach them not just books and tests,
But how to live with hearts at rest.
To care for self and those who raised,
To walk with kindness all their days.
Guide them with wisdom, strong yet kind,
To know true wealth is peace of mind.
In a world that's often loud and fast,
Show them what it means to last.
Let them learn to cherish life,
Beyond mere gain, beyond the strife.
To find joy in the simplest things,
And understand what love can bring.
For life is more than a blind race,
Not just a chase for fleeting grace.
Teach them to seek a deeper goal,
To nurture both the heart and soul.
True success is more than gold,
It's living wisely, growing old.
With lessons learned and love to share,
A life well-lived, beyond compare.

12. Circle

In childhood's light, we grew so free,
With arms, a canopy,
Their laughter rang, their love so bright,
A shelter in the darkest night.
They watched us soar, they watched us play,
In every step, their hearts would stay.
Years flew by, like leaves in wind,
And we grew up, as life begins,
Their hair turned silver-white,
Their steps grew slower, day to night.
Yet still they smiled, with tender grace,
Their love, a never-fading place.
But time, relentless, takes its due,
The day arrived when skies turned blue,
Their hands that held us, now felt weak,
Their voices soft, with words they speak.
We feel the ache, the silent pain,
Of losing love we'll never gain.
The umbrella gone, no more the shade,
Of those who loved, and softly prayed,
Their warmth, their care, now memories,
They were a gentle breeze.

How deep the sorrow, how vast the void,
In hearts where joy and grief collide.
Oh, how I wish that love could stay,
Memories never fade away,
The bonds of blood and bonds of heart,
Would never break, or drift apart.
Our growth was their dream,
In every laugh, their love redeemed.
Now it's our turn to hold the light,
To guide the young day and night,
To give the love that we received,
To weave the dreams they weaved.
A circle turning, never done,
In every child, a love begun.

13. An Angel Warrior

An angel, light of our home,
A radiant gift from heaven above,
She fills our days with joy and grace,
A pure reflection of boundless love.
Her laughter dances like morning sun,
Her spirit brightens every room,
She is the heart that holds us close,
The gentle wind that chases gloom.
In her eyes, we find a world of dreams,
A future bright, a path untold,
She is the essence of tender strength,
A story that's meant to unfold.
She is closest to a father's heart,
Soft as petals, strong as trees,
Delicate yet brave, they shine so bright,
The purest form of femininity.
Adore her like a goddess, with reverence and pride,
For she carries the power of creation's spark,
Her spirit flows like a river wide,
Guiding us through both light and dark.
Yet, teach her to be fierce and bold,
To stand her ground and speak her mind,

For not all are taught to honor her light,
In a world where respect is sometimes blind.
And sons, teach them the value of grace,
To see in her their equal part,
Respecting her as divine,
Is where we build a kinder heart.

14. A Life Well Lived

To live a life where love is sown,
And look back proud, with no regrets shown,
To know you've spread kindness wide and clear,
Is to leave this world with a heart sincere.

15. Enduring

In the beginning, they're strangers, truth be told,
Two rough-edged sandpapers, each with a separate hold,
Rubbing and wearing, in a dance somewhat rough,
Learning slowly that love is both tender and tough.
But as the years pass, the rough edges wear thin,
They find in each other a true friend within.
When children move on, their own lives to chart,
They draw closer together, two halves of one heart.
Now hand in hand, they walk through life's twilight,
May God keep them together, day into night.
For each one depends on the other's warm grace,
Together forever, in love's sweet embrace.

16. Sea of Feeling

In this vast sea of feelings deep,
Some honor, some forget to keep.
One holds struggles close,
With lifelong respect, their love they chose.
Joy lights up the their eyes,
A beacon in the ever-changing skies.
Yet others drift on distant tides,
The sacrifices cast aside.
In silent pain, they yearn,
For love unreturned, a heart's concern.
In this sea of feeling, the waves do show,
How love's warmth blooms, or cold winds blow.

17. Empowerment

Feminine energy, the world's true force,
Strong and pure, our guiding course.
Shakti, life's essence, creation's hand,
Moves mountains, shapes the land.
In every woman, this power resides,
A strength unseen, yet vast and wide.
She births the stars, stirs the seas,
Her spirit breathes in all we see.
As Shiva honors Shakti's might,
We must cherish her day and night.
When Shakti leads and Shiva guides,
Love and peace will always thrive.

18. Essentials of Today

In today's world, two things matter most:
Family, the foundation of support and love,
And savings, the cushion that prepares us for life's ups and downs.
Value your loved ones and manage your riches wisely,
These are the keys to a stable and fulfilling life.
In nurturing relationships and securing your future,
You build a life that is both rich and meaningful.

19. Borderless

Why build these borders that make us fight,
When love can cross in a single flight
No wall is strong, no line too wide,
To keep apart hearts open wide.
In land, beneath, sky,
The same sun sets, the same stars sigh.
Why not let love dissolve the line,
And hold the world in a shared design

20. Seed

Plant a seed in humble earth,
Watch it sprout, a new life's birth.
A garden grown with tender care,
Brings joy and peace beyond compare.
Just as a seed holds a tree within,
Learn from it where true growth begins.
Nurture dreams with patience and grace,
For in every seed, a future takes its place.

21. Mind Openers

From revered's words, we learn to see,
The wisdom in humility,
Their guidance roots us, helps us grow,
A path of truth, a steady glow.
Through distant lands, our spirits roam,
Each journey broadens thoughts of home,
New faces, places, sights unknown,
Expand the heart, the seeds are sown.
In reads and pals, we find the keys,
To open minds, to set them free,
With every page, with every voice,
We learn to live, we learn to choice.

22. Deeds of Success

Plant a tree and let it grow,
A simple act, a future's glow.
Write something to light the way,
A gift of wisdom that will stay.
To raise a child with love and grace,
Is to illuminate the world as a brighter place.

23. A Life Well Lived

To walk this loved ones with joy in stride,
To find our peace, let the heart decide,
With open skies and spirits light,
We seek the sun, embrace its light.
To give our love, both near and far,
A gentle touch, a guiding star,
In every smile, in every deed,
We plant the world with kindness' seed.
And when our time has come to rest,
May we depart with hearts at best,
With grace, we leave the world we know,
A quiet farewell, a peaceful glow.

24. Illuminated

In music's realm where notes take flight,
Your melodies soar, a dance of light,
Each chord a spark in the vast expanse,
A bridge to stars where dreams enhance.

Oh, luminous souls you chase the divine,
In your craft, the universe aligns,
Through music, art, and every game,
You touch the heavens, and call their name.

In art's embrace where colors sing,
You paint the light of the cosmic ring,
Each stroke a whisper from the skies,
A canvas where the boundless lies.
Oh, luminous souls you chase the divine.

In sport, where motion meets the grace,
Your spirit dances in a cosmic space,
Each leap and strike, a divine flow,
In every move, the heavens show.
Oh, luminous souls you chase the divine.

So rise and shine with hearts so bright,
Your gifts a beacon in the night,
In every beat,art and every play,
You bring the light of the heavens' way.

25. The Shadows of Desire

Desire, a relentless force, clouds the mind with yearning,
Its endless demands twist joy into suffering,
Chasing after illusions, we weave chains around our hearts,
Each unfulfilled longing becomes a shadow of our own making.
To master desire is to embrace a stillness beyond craving,
In the quiet restraint of our deepest wants, true peace unfolds.
When we temper our desires, the illusions dissipate,
And the wonders of contentment reveal themselves, unobstructed.

The Shadows of Desire - 2

Desire is a chasm that swallows the heart,
Its insatiable hunger cloaks us in illusion,
We chase after phantoms of wealth, love, and power,
Each unfulfilled wish becomes a wound, deep and unending.
To transcend desire is to step into a realm of profound stillness,
Where true contentment arises from the freedom of inner restraint.
In tempering our cravings, we release the chains that bind us,

And the true essence of peace and wonder unfurls, boundless and clear.

26. Silence?

They came, tender as dawn breaking over a darkened field,
With words soft as feathers, strong as iron—
The beacons, the messengers, bearers of truth, love and peace,
Sent to soothe the weary, to heal the broken,
Their wisdom like water for a parched earth.
They offered us their hands, their hearts,
Paths of light carved through the chaos of life,
And promised: follow, and you will find peace,
Grow in spirit, become whole.
They were the supreme, the true, the divine.
But what demons do we harbor in our souls?
What madness grips us that we cannot bear
The sight of such purity, such unwavering grace?
We have silenced their voices with blood,
Cast them from our midst with blades and scourges,
Made them sit on hot plates, tortured them with nails,
Made martyrs of them,
While their truths still echo in our guilty skies.
In every corner of this wide, weary world,
Across cultures, across time,
We have repeated the sin, the crime,
To kill what we do not understand,

To destroy what we fear to embrace.
And still, their words remain,
Etched in the sacred scrolls,
Carved into our memories,
Echoing in our prayers and hymns.
But do we hear them, truly?
Or are they just whispers in the wind,
Lost in the noise of our unending chaos?
Centuries have passed like sands through a sieve,
And what have we learned?
The earth still trembles with war and hate,
The children of God still walk in shadow,
And the heavens weep for the family
That bore such gifts only to bury them.
If we were to meet them now,
In the light beyond this fractured world,
How would we show our faces?
What could we say to the ones we crucified,
To the mothers and fathers who gave us such love?
Would we stand silent, ashamed,
Or finally confess: We were blind,
We were lost, we were fools,
And now, we seek the way home.
But can we ever return
From a path so dark, so stained?
Or are we forever the lost children
Of a world that never accepted to listen?

And in the end, will we be remembered
As the killers of saints,
Or the ones who finally,
With trembling hands and tear-streaked faces,
Reached out to grasp the light
That was always within our reach?

27. Elegant

In the wild, where shadows softly creep,
A leopard's grace through the forest sweeps.
Highly adaptive, it dances with the trees,
Its sleek, spotted coat blending with ease.
Intelligent eyes that scan and scheme,
A master of stealth, a wildlifer's dream.
With strength unmatched, it leaps so high,
A silent whisper through the moonlit sky.
Climbing branches, it surveys the land,
A planner with a cunning hand.
Jim Corbett's admiration rings true,
For this majestic beast in every hue.
Speed like lightning, a blur in the night,
Jumping with power, a spectacular sight.
Its hunting prowess, a dance of might,
In solitude, it finds its light.
In the urban sprawl, it still impresses,
A symbol of strength that never compresses.
A spiritual guide in its quiet grace,
Even in cities, it finds its sacred space.
In wild or city, it roams with pride,
A testament to nature's wondrous guide.

Leopard's legacy, a tale of lore,
A creature of awe forevermore.
Humans must accept and be aware,
Respect its realm, for it's rare and fair.

28. Majesty

The land's grandeur the jungle's embrace,
Giants walk with a timeless grace.
Their wisdom deep, their spirits grand,
A lesson for humanity to understand.
Strong and gentle, they lead with might,
In matriarchal bonds, they shine bright.
A society built on care and respect,
Where every member's needs are met.
Emotional depth in every gaze,
Compassion flows in their gentle ways.
With trunks that hug and soothe the distressed,
In times of sorrow, they stand true and undressed.
Memory vast as the ocean's tide,
They remember paths and kins with pride.
A testament to intelligence rare,
An intricate dance of love and care.
They mourn the dead with a heartfelt grace,
Expressing emotions in their own embrace.
Joy, anger, fear, and love they show,
In every gesture, their feelings flow.
Humanity claims a crown so bright,
Yet often fails to grasp the light.

For to call oneself the best of all,
One must learn from those who heed nature's call.
From elephants, learn the strength in tears,
The power of empathy through the years.
Yet we, who claim to be wise and grand,
Slay these beings with brutal hand.
Ruthless with those who teach us to care,
We tarnish our claim, a truth laid bare.
How can we call ourselves truly humane,
When we destroy the best, in vain?

29. Letter to Frost

Dear Robert Frost,

In fleeting years, the world has changed, its verdant canvasses laid bare,
Our cities sprawl where once were woods, in heedless haste and dire despair.
The earth, once lush with nature's grace, now bears the marks of human tread,
A testament to dreams eroded, by the weight of progress' dread.
In your tranquil verse, "Stopping by Woods on a Snowy Evening,"
We find the woods you once revered, now marred by time's unfeeling scheming.
We yearn to halt, to linger long, and drink the forest's silent plea,
To savor still its pristine charm, and dream of what it used to be.
Yet, as you wrote, "And miles to go before I sleep," we seek to pause,
To dwell amidst the woods' embrace, and heal the scars we've caused.
In "The Road Not Taken," we seek the wisdom that your lines bestow,
As our generation wanders lost, through paths of doubt and choices slow.
We falter at the crossroads stark, directionless in this new age,

Desiring guidance through the mist, to chart our course upon life's stage.
Teach us to choose with steadfast heart, to brave the missteps we may face,
And know that every turn we make reveals another path, a new embrace.
With gratitude profound and deep, for poems timeless, true, and bright,
We thank you, Frost, for guiding us through every shadowed night.
May your verses, rich and resonant, continue to inspire and renew,
In a world that seeks both truth and light, and yearns for visions clear and true.
Please write more...
Yours sincerely,

30. Pausing by Woods in Every Season

Whose woods these are, I surely know.
A gift they are, where life does grow.
Their owner's far, his home in town,
Yet here they stand, a world renowned.
The woods are deep, and dark, and wide,
A refuge where the spirits bide.
I pause within their silent grace,
And let the world slow down its pace.
In spring, they bloom with vibrant green,
In summer's warmth, a cool serene.
Autumn's hues in fiery glow,
Winter's blanket pure as snow.
Yet more than seasons' shifting light,
These woods hold peace both day and night.
Men leave with promises to keep,
To guard these woods and their roots deep.
And miles to go before I sleep,
Yet in these woods, my heart will keep.
The joy, the calm, the ancient will,
To save these woods for all, until.

31. Begin Anew

Two paths diverged in a quiet wood,
And sorry I could not walk both,
And be one traveler, long I stood
And gazed down one as far as I could
To where it bent in the undergrowth.
Then took the other, just as fair,
And having perhaps the better claim,
Because it was grassy and wanted wear;
Though as for that, the passing there
Had worn them really about the same.
And both that morning equally lay
In leaves no step had trodden black.
Oh, I kept the first for another day!
Yet knowing how way leads on to way,
I doubted if I should ever come back.
But here's the truth I've come to see:
If I should find I've lost my way,
No step too late, no need to stray
I'll turn around, or set it free—
A new path made from what might be,
For wrong decisions should not cause dismay.

I shall be telling this with a sigh
Somewhere ages and ages hence:
Two paths diverged in a wood, and I—
I took a turn, and if it went awry,
I made a new one, and moved on by.

Gratitude

As you close the final pages of *Whispers of Life*, I want to extend my deepest thanks to you, the reader. Your journey through these messages has breathed life into this collection, transforming it from a series of words into a shared experience of love, reflection, and discovery.

Thank you for embracing the themes of this book—love, nature, and the wild dance between them. Your willingness to delve into the whispers of life, to connect with the emotions and imagery within these pages, has made this journey profoundly meaningful.

To love—thank you for being the guiding light throughout this work. The love of family, friends, and the enduring bonds that shape our lives have been the heart of these words. Your support, encouragement, and inspiration have been instrumental in bringing these words to life.

And to the wild, which has been both a muse and a mentor—thank you for the lessons learned and the beauty observed. The natural world, with its untamed splendor and quiet strength, has infused these pages with its wisdom and wonder. Your presence in this book is a tribute to the resilience and grace of the creatures and landscapes that continue to inspire and captivate.

It is my hope that *Whispers of Life* has inspired you to listen to the whispers around you, to cherish the love in your life, and to appreciate the wild that sustain us. Your engagement with this book has been a profound reminder of the interconnectedness of all things, and for that, I am truly grateful.

With heartfelt appreciation and warmest regards,

Navdeep Sood

www.ingramcontent.com/pod-product-compliance
Lightning Source LLC
LaVergne TN
LVHW040919150826
845672LV00007B/2108

9798895881002